I0461759

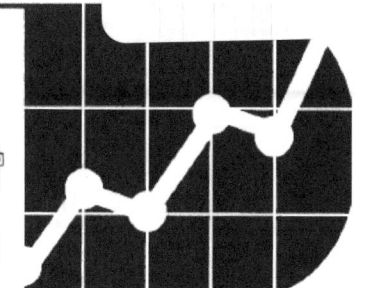

Performance Management
Practitioner Series

Improving Customer Service
Through
Effective Performance
Management

United States Performance
Office of Management
Personnel and Incentive   PMD-04
Management Awards Division   September 1997

Table of Contents

Introduction

On September 7, 1993, President Clinton set the Federal Government on the path to high-quality customer service by issuing Execu tive Order 12862, "Setting Customer Service Standards" (see Appendix 1). Through this order, the President has set the goal for Federal agencies to deliver customer service that equals the best in business.

Agency response to the President's order is described in *Putting Customers First: Standards for Serving the American People,* a Report of the National Performance Review (NPR). This NPR report, published in September 1994, presents more than 1,500 customer service standards, representing goals and standards set by more than 100 Federal agencies.

On March 22, 1995, the President again focused attention on improving customer service when he issued a memorandum for heads of executive departments and agencies that addressed the second phase of reinventing government (see Appendix 2). In that memo, he advises agencies to integrate customer service measures with other performance initiatives and to align employee appraisal and recognition programs with a customer focus.

A concern about the quality of service to its customers is not new in the Government. The statute that sets forth requirements for employee performance appraisal at section 4302(b) of title 5, United States Code, specifically mentions "the extent of courtesy demonstrated to the public" as a possible criterion for evaluating job performance.

Another requirement for agencies to set goals comes from the Government Performance and Results Act (the Results Act) of 1993. The Results Act requires agencies to develop organizational performance plans, establish performance goals that are objective and measurable, establish performance indicators to be used in measuring outputs, service levels, and outcomes of each program, and submit performance reports to the Office of Management and Budget. The organizational performance management system established at the agency level through the Results Act is similar to the employee performance man-agement system agencies establish under Governmentwide regulation in 5 CFR 430. Both include establishing performance plans, setting goals, developing measurement systems, and assessing performance.

Because individual performance management plans should align individual and team performance goals to the goals of the agency, both Executive Order 12862 and the Results Act should have a significant effect on agency performance management programs.

This paper describes how agencies can use their employee performance management systems as tools to help them reach the customer service goals they've set under Executive Order 12862 and the Results Act. Throughout the paper, references to performance management and its component processes will apply at the individual or team level unless otherwise noted. The terms "standard" and "goal" are also used throughout this paper. A special discussion of those terms follows.

A Note on Terminology: Standards and Goals

The terms *"standards"* and *"goals"* are used throughout this paper and in related literature and general practice. These terms have no precise or standard definition. Sometimes they are used synonymously, and at other times they are used with connotations that establish a contrast between the terms. In the interest of limiting confusion, the context and connotations of these terms are discussed here, and a convention is established for how the terms will be used in this paper.

Within the Government's performance management system, the concept of a performance standard first appears as a fundamental feature in law. The term is included in the statutory definition of "unacceptable performance," which is defined at 5 U.S.C. 4301(3) as "performance that fails to meet **established performance standards**." This notion of a standard describing the minimally acceptable level of performance is common in literature and practice concerning performance appraisal. Sometimes the term *"retention standard"* is used as a more explicit description of this connotation of "standard," consistent with the application in Government that unacceptable performance may be used as the basis for a demotion or removal action.

In the context of the current performance appraisal system, a somewhat broader use of the term "performance standard" is also found. The Governmentwide performance management regulations define "performance standard" as "the management-approved expression of the performance threshold(s), requirement(s), or expectation(s) that must be met to be appraised at **a particular level of performance**." A separate standard may be established for each level of performance, including the "Outstanding" level. Clearly, performance that fails to reach an established performance standard that defines "Outstanding" performance would not be considered "Unacceptable" performance.

The idea of using a "standard" to define a level of performance well above a "retention standard" has other applications beyond formal appraisal. This connotation of "desirable" or **"target performance"** was used in the Executive Order on setting customer service standards. In describing their customer service standards, many agencies are establishing a *"goal"* for a future level of performance that has yet to be reached. Here, failure to meet a customer service standard should certainly stimulate management and employee attention and commitment to improving performance and reaching the performance goal. Yet such failure should not necessarily be labeled "Unacceptable" performance and prompt actions like demotions, removals, or even within-grade increase denials.

Applying these two ideas and connotations in combination offers a powerful performance management tool. The (retention) standard and goal for a given area of performance together define an **acceptable range of performance**. (See Figure 1.) Falling below that range is unacceptable. Achieving performance above that range is exceptional.

Organizations have found that establishing such a range of acceptable performance between the standard and the goal can be a very effective way to communicate performance expectations and can raise employee performance levels.

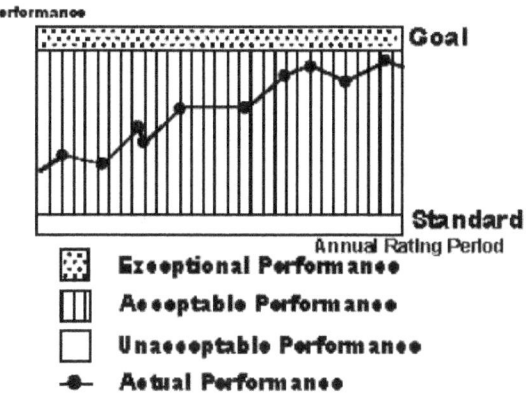

Figure 1

In contrast, some organizations use an approach where an all-purpose standard is set. If the standard is set high, that standard essentially reflects a goal, rather than establishing a range of acceptable performance. (See Figure 2.) A single target has been set, which in its retention standard context may be arbitrarily and unreasonably high. If the standard is set too low, it offers no challenge for improvement. When such a **single standard/goal** is established, there may be a tendency to use that target as an evaluation and punishment tool, rather than as a tool to promote performance improvement.

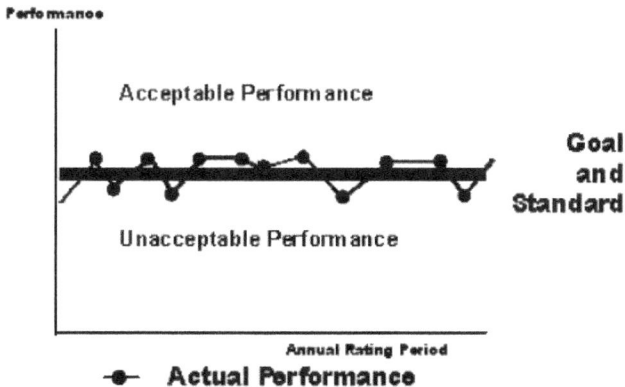

Figure 2

Throughout this paper, unless otherwise noted, the term *"standard"* will be limited to its "retention standard" connotation, and the term *"goal"* will be used when a "performance target" is being discussed.

Performance Management's Components

A successful performance management program supports and promotes the accomplishment of an agency's mission and goals. An effective program includes four key components:

1. setting individual and team goals that are aligned with the agency's goals;
2. establishing a measurement system that is accepted by users;
3. providing adequate, timely feedback; and
4. rewarding and recognizing desired performance.

If each of these components is designed with customer satisfaction as the focus, the performance management program will promote the agency's customer service goals and improve individual and agency performance. Considering and redesigning these four key components independently will not improve performance as effectively as when they are examined and coordinated in tandem.

The rest of this paper addresses each of these four processes and how they can be linked for effective performance management that supports agency customer service goals.

Component ❶:
Setting Customer Service Standards and Goals

Goal setting is the first component of effective performance management. Individual and team customer service goals should be aligned with the agency's customer service goals established through Executive Order 12862 and the Results Act. If they are not, time, money, and energy will be channeled in the wrong direction and it is unlikely that the agency will provide best-in-business customer service.

Research on Goal Setting.

Setting appropriate individual standards and goals is extremely important for the effective performance of individuals and teams. Research has shown that if goals are too low or too high, the motivation and commitment level of employees is low (Connellan & Zemke, 1993). Research has also shown that specific, hard goals result in higher performance than vague or abstract goals or no goals at all. Further, specific hard goals that are accepted by employees result in higher performance than easy goals (Locke & Latham, 1984).

Other research on goal setting has shown that feedback regarding one's past performance does not lead to improved future performance unless the feedback leads to or is accompanied by a goal for improved performance. In performance appraisal sessions, for example, Locke and Latham found that People who are given feedback perform no better than those who receive no feedback. However, when goal setting takes place as a result of the feedback, performance improves significantly. Both goals and feedback are necessary to produce and sustain positive performance change.

Locke and Latham also observe that goals affect performance by means of three major mechanisms:
1. goals direct an individual's thoughts and actions;
2. goals regulate energy expenditure; and
3. hard goals that are accepted by an individual increase that individual's persistence in achieving the goal.

When goals are customer-focused, employee thoughts and actions are centered on customer satisfaction, effort is expended to satisfy customers, and employees will continue to strive to please customers when the goal is challenging and they've agreed to the goal.

Finally, Locke and Latham observed that employee involvement in setting the goal increases the chance of acceptance of the goal by the employee, although employee involvement alone does not improve performance.

Who Are Our Customers?

Before agencies can set their organization-wide customer service goals, they must determine who their customers are. Customers are found both outside and within the agency. Due to the wide variety of missions within the scope of the Federal government, each Federal agency may have a different set of customers. Employees and teams within each agency may also have a variety of customers. Methods and sources for identifying customer identity could include surveys, user lists, stakeholders, correspondence, submitted forms or applications, and employees themselves.

Internal Customers. Internal customers should not be overlooked. Providing high-quality internal customer service can improve the ability of an agency to satisfy external customers. Employees in administrative support positions, for instance, may service internal customers. According to T. Kerry McCarter, vice president of quality management at Johnson & Johnson's Quality Institute, "Internal customer service is meeting the expectations and requirements for success of those people inside the company so they can delight customers in the marketplace" (Azzolini and Shillaber, 1993).

Organizations with excellent external and poor internal customer service are often performing on the edge of acceptability. For example, an organization that has a poor computer support section in its administrative division may find that their customer service representatives cannot get vital information to their customers because the computers never work.

Setting Goals and Defining Standards.

Customer service goals and standards must not be set arbitrarily, but should be established based on customer research data (Goodman, 1993). This is true at both the agency level and the individual level. Too often management will use intuition to set customer service standards and goals. A huge gap often exists between management's conception and what is actually important to customers. Rather, agencies should depend on empirical data gathered from the customers themselves to determine the goals of the organization, its teams, and its individuals.

Goals must also be measurable and verifiable. If you can't quantify or verify performance in reaching the goal, there will be no way to assess levels of performance or specify where improvement is needed.

Using Customer Research To Identify Goals. Asking customers what they want is the most important part of setting customer service standards and goals both at the agency level and the individual level (Connellan and Zemke, 1993). Methods for determining customer needs include one-on-one interviews of key customers, focus groups, polling front-line service employees, questionnaires that allow for employee comments, and key decision maker mini-groups that pull together the major stakeholders of the agency's services. Using a variety of these methods will provide a laundry list of customer issues. From this list, the agency could distill a meaningful set of attributes that define quality for its customers (Flanagan and Fredericks, 1993). Once a list of attributes is established, an agency would define measures of key performance indicators and measure current baseline performance against customer-desired performance. It should then work the results of that analysis into agency performance standards and goals (Wilson, 1993)

Once customer research has been done and agency goals are established, managers and employees can align team and individual standards and goals with the agency's goals. This may require additional customer research that will be more focused on specific work processes, services, or products. For example, if an agency's customer service goal is to make its publications easy to understand, a team or an individual may want to determine customer needs for written materials and then test the final products with customer focus groups to determine if they are easily understood.

Example of Customer Research. Developing and improving customer service standards is vital to performance improvement, from the agency level to the individual level. One example of an organization that studied customer satisfaction and set service performance standards accordingly is Florida Power and Light (FPL).

FPL conducted a detailed study on customer satisfaction and phone queues for customer service. They found that the average time customers expected to wait on the phone for a customer representative without knowing the length of the wait was 94 seconds. Because of high levels of customer calls, company representatives were unable to consistently meet that 94-second time frame. The company found that the longer the wait, the lower the customers rated the performance of the company representatives.

To help manage customer expectations, and as a way of establishing more realistic levels of expected performance for their customer representatives, FPL established a phone queue device called "Smartqueue" that periodically informed waiting customers how much longer they had to wait for a company representative to answer the phone. The company found that when the customers knew the length of the wait, they were willing to wait an average of 105 seconds longer (a total of 199 seconds). FPL was able to translate these customer requirements into target service levels (standards and goals) for each segment of their customer population. "Smartqueue" was rated helpful by 99 percent of customers through a customer survey. The mean satisfaction rating for those waiting less than one minute was 1.29 where "1" was equal to "extremely satisfied" and "5" was "extremely unsatisfied" (Graessel and Zeidler, 1993).

Performance Plans Based on Goals. Individual performance plans, which can include both retention-level standards and target-level goals, should be reviewed carefully at the beginning of the performance period to ensure that plans are aligned with agency goals. Evaluating the proposed plans also allows managers, teams, and individuals to determine the feasibility of attaining the goals that were set. For example, it might be discovered that no suitable individual performance plans can be developed for a particular goal because the individual cannot control the inputs needed to attain it. In such a case, the goal may need to be revised to either apply to a larger group, such as the team or division, or to be rewritten so that outside factors are excluded. For example, it would be inappropriate to establish the following goal for a critical element in an employee's performance plan:

Element: Customer Service
Outstanding Standard: The Region will complete 30 case reviews per week.

The employee has no control over the entire Region's case completion rate. (And critical elements may only address individual performance.) A more appropriate performance standard at the outstanding level for a critical element might look like this:

> **Element:** Completing Customer Cases
> **Outstanding Standard:** The employee completes either two simple cases or a moderately difficult case per week. A completed case includes all required documents, accurate recommendations, and valid information.

Benefits of Goal Setting.

Setting goals offers many advantages. In their seminal work on goal setting, Locke and Latham (1984) suggest that:

- Goals can clarify employee expectations about desired performance. Possibly one of the best ways to clarify customer service goals that are based on customer research is to have the employees do the research themselves. This gives them a greater knowledge of customer needs and expectations, and how the goals were set.

- Setting goals can relieve boredom in monotonous jobs. The authors give the example of a person directed to knock down several pins with a ball over a hun-dred times a day. The job soon becomes boring. But give the person the goal to try to knock down as many pins as possible in each shot, or even to try to hit all ten pins down in each shot, and the task soon becomes an interesting game bowling!

- When people attain goals and receive feedback indicating that the goals have been reached, they feel increased liking for the task and satisfaction with their performance on the job they are doing. This can especially apply to attaining customer service goals and receiving feedback from satisfied customers.

- Feedback on goal accomplishment provides the employee with recognition by peers, supervisors, and coaches.

- Setting and achieving goals increases self-confidence, pride in achievement, and increased willingness to accept future challenges as a result of goal setting.

- Participative goal setting has been found to be effective in increasing performance and in generating feelings of competency among employees who are uneducated, who have a weak ego, and/or a negative self-image.

Pitfalls of Goal Setting.

Locke and Latham acknowledge often-cited arguments against goal setting. They offer rebuttals to those arguments that apply parti-cularly well to customer service goals:

- Goals may tend to be set only for those aspects of performance that are easily measurable (such as number of phone calls answered per day) but goals can be set for any verifiable activity or behavior (such as customer phone requests answered effectively and politely).

- Goals may emphasize only short-term performance (so many applications pro-cessed per week) but there is no reason long-term goals cannot be set (such as streamlining the application process).

- Goals may promote undue risk-taking (such as purchasing new computer software that has not been used by the agency before) but this may be mitigated by a proper risk analysis (doing a thorough evaluation and specification check before the purchase is made).

- Goals may increase stress (employees may be worried about not being able to reach the goal)—but goals may also reduce stress by eliminating role conflict and ambiguity (employees will know what is expected of them).

- Failure to attain goals can reduce motivation—but credit can be given for partial success by making the goals challenging yet reachable for carefully selected and trained employees and by emphasizing performance or improvement rather than goal attainment. For example, if a single target standard/goal is set arbitrarily high and the employee does not meet the target, there is no range of acceptable performance within which to credit the performance they did achieve. If, however, both a target goal and a retention standard are set, recognizing employees for their achievements above the retention level standard will let them know that their efforts are appreciated. And it will encourage them to improve their performance further.

- Goals may be treated as ceilings on performance (due to fear of adverse consequences if goals are exceeded). For example, some employees may fear that jobs may be lost if production goals are reached or if it appears that fewer employees are needed because of improved agency performance. This usually implies a lack of trust in management by

employees. To combat this, agencies should develop a climate of mutual respect and supportiveness and foster good two-way communication.

Some Sage Advice.

George S. Easton, an experienced Baldrige award examiner, has developed a list of common organizational performance weaknesses. Customer service standards and goals is one area that is often poor. He states that in most of the total quality organizations that he's examined, customer service standards are not well defined except in cases where there are easy and obvious mea-sures. He also observes that methods for assessing customer service performance rela-tive to standards are generally poor. He recommends a management-by-fact approach that uses improved customer research tech-niques for setting standards and goals, and better measurement systems (Easton, 1993).

Locke and Latham (1984) also provide a word of advice on the use of goals when they observe—

"We cannot overemphasize the fact that the purpose of goal setting is to increase a person's motivation. But goal setting can have the opposite effect if it is used primarily as a yardstick for documenting a person's failures. Goal setting should be used as a guide, as an incentive to increase performance, and as a means of promoting pride in accomplishment."

Component ❷: Measurement System

Measuring or quantifying customer needs, expectations, and satisfaction is a basic requirement for customer-focused performance management programs for two reasons: first, for determining where to set standards and goals, and second, for providing a means of feedback to employees and teams on their efforts to reach their goals. Effective customer research for setting goals hinges on measuring the issues that are truly important to customers. These types of measures focus on the results that the customer wants, such as a product or service. On the other hand, effective feedback measurements provide information on the process of supplying the product or service so that individuals and teams will know where improvements can be made. Both purposes of measurement should be addressed to ensure customer satisfaction.

In addition, objective, customer-based measurement systems will enable an agency to align its improvement efforts with customer opinions and priorities, leading to the best use of its resources. By involving employees at every level, customer research creates an internal climate that cultivates employee commitment to customer service. Customer-satisfaction research translates into improved customer satisfaction, and improves internal management efficiency.

Steps for Developing a Measurement System.

When developing a measurement system, whether it is to be applied at the agency or individual level, it is important to include the following steps:

1. Identify the goals that need to be measured. (Goals should be specific and measurable as noted above.)

2. Develop performance indicators to measure the products, services and/or outcomes established in the goal setting process.

3. Involve employees. Involvement is important for developing trust in the measures. Employees will be more like-
ly to accept and be committed to reaching goals tracked by measures that they have been involved in developing.

4. Use multiple measures and inputs. A single measure will usually not adequately describe the full range of performance.

5. Provide flexibility. The measurement system should be sufficiently flexible to allow for change.

6. Provide for feedback. The measurement system should provide adequate feedback to agencies, teams, and individuals on performance. Feedback promotes performance improvement.

7. Analyze the data to ensure that an accurate meaning of the results is derived.

8. Be patient. Performance improvement and measurement improvement is a

long-term process—management patience is needed.

Customer-Focused Measures.

Categories of customer satisfaction measures are listed below as examples. These measures may be used first to determine standards and goals and then used to monitor and improve performance.

Result or Outcome Measures. Results measures tell agencies, teams, and individuals where they stand in their efforts to achieve goals (Meyer, 1994). For customer service standards and goals, measuring the number of customer complaints, compliments, awards received from customers, and recommendations by customers to others will indicate customer satisfaction with the service or product. Customer satisfaction measures also could include comparing the final product or service to the customer's requirements, i.e., was the customer's order for supplies or products complete and delivered on time. Examples of result or outcome measures include:

- A small museum that has a goal to increase patronage as well as to retain long-term customers might measure the number of new visitors and the percentage of repeat visitors through the use of a sign-in book.

- If the customer service goal of a map distribution team is to fill the orders of customers correctly and to ship within 5 working days, the team might monitor customer complaints, order correction requests, and order shipment time.

- The customer service goal of a position classifier may be to keep position descriptions up-to-date so that the human

resource team can accomplish its goal of achieving quicker staffing response. The classifier could establish a tracking or tickler system that ranks the position descriptions in order of need for review.

Process Measures. Process measures monitor the tasks and activities that produce a given result (Meyer, 1994). Process measures might include cycle time, error rate, wasted time or supplies, and other activities specific to the type of work. Examples of process measures include:

- An agency might want to analyze its customer correspondence process by measuring the time it takes to respond to the customer and the steps needed (such as approval and review) to get the correspondence in the mail.

- A team responsible for printing agency publications might want to measure the error rate and down time of their copying machines to determine the best machines for future purchases.

- Individuals responsible for reviewing claims might want to track the number of cases they process weekly or monthly.

Using a Process Flowchart to Identify Process Measures.

One way that many organizations determine key process measurements is to develop a flow chart of an entire work process. The flow chart enables organizations to pinpoint which part of the process should be measured in order to make improvements.

One example of the successful use of process flowcharting that focused on increasing customer satisfaction comes from the Boise Cascade Timber and Wood Products Division in Boise, Idaho. Boise's customers were unhappy with the time they had to wait for orders. In an effort to increase customer satisfaction, Boise Cascade measured and documented the time taken for notifying and scheduling their lumber-ready loads and for preparing truck-ready shipments from the mill. One area of performance that flow-charting showed was adding significant time to the orders was how status requests by customers were handled. The time it took to locate orders, communicate with truckers, and respond to customers was measured in detail. Measuring the lost time for each step gave managers and employees specific information as to where they needed to improve. Further, by analyzing the entire process they were able to cut 52 steps down to 7 steps, and waiting days for customers from 3.25 days to 1.39 days, thus increasing customer satisfaction (Pratt, 1993).

Measuring Customer Dissatisfaction.

Knowing why customers are dissatisfied with agency services will provide guidance to managers and employees for areas of improvement. Studies show that, on the average

across all industries (including Government) about 50 percent of all customers with problems or questions never complain to anyone. Approximately 45 percent complain to someone at a frontline level, and only 5 percent (or less) actually contact headquarters (Goodman, et al, 1993). Managers and teams using customer complaints as results measures can use this data to estimate total customer dissatisfaction and to improve customer dissatisfaction measurement tools.

Furthermore, studies have shown that the customers who complain and receive satisfaction often exhibit no less, and sometimes greater, loyalty than the customers who did not experience a problem. In Government, although customers cannot necessarily switch brands, they can demand extra services, become repeat complainants, or escalate their complaint to members of Congress or regulating agencies. This suggests that failure to meet customer expectations (defined by the customer's experience of problems) results in a significant cost to the Government and the taxpayers (Goodman et al,. 1993). If agencies focus on customer complaint resolution as well as improving customer service, they can improve long-term customer satisfaction.

Component ❸:
Feedback

Feedback is the third component of a successful and effective performance management program. Research has shown that individuals who receive feedback on performance relative to their goals will be more committed to their goals than individuals who do not receive feedback. Effective customer service feedback is:

Specific. Feedback works best when it relates to a specific goal. Establishing employee performance goals before work begins is the key to providing tangible, objective, and powerful feedback. Telling employees that they are doing well because they exceeded their goal by servicing 10 percent more customers is more effective than simply saying "you're doing a good job."

Timely. To have an effective customer service program, employees need feedback on a day-to-day basis regarding their performance on reaching their customer service goals. If improvement needs to be made in their performance, the sooner they find out about it, the sooner they can correct the problem. If employees have reached or exceeded a goal, the sooner they receive positive feedback, the more rewarding it is to them.

Appropriate. Feedback should be given in an appropriate manner that will help improve performance best. Since people respond better to information presented in a positive way, feedback should be expressed in a positive manner. This is not to say that it should be sugar-coated. It must be accurate, factual, and complete. When

presented, however, feedback is more effective when it reinforces what the employee did right and then identifies what needs to be done in the future. Constant criticism eventually will fall upon deaf ears.

Sources of Feedback.

Performance feedback on customer service goals can come from the following sources:

Customers are the most important source of feedback for customer service performance. Since the Executive order requires agencies to solicit customer feedback on each of their programs' performance, groups, teams, and individuals can use that data as it applies to their specific program areas. They can also develop feedback tools to gather information about more specific performance, even to the individual level. However, it may not be appropriate to gather information directly from customers on specific employee performance. For example, if the nature of the work itself causes customer dissatisfaction (such as tax or compliance examining), customers may rate employees low because of the process itself and not the employee's performance.

Work measurement systems, such as statistical process control measures, supply information to agencies, teams and employees to update them on performance and to indicate areas for improvement.

Supervisors, managers, and team leaders can give employees feedback on the agency's overall customer service performance and also provide specific feedback on individual and team performance in meeting particular goals.

Peers can be a valuable source of information about individual performance, especially when work is interdependent. They may have a better overall picture of the employee's performance, particularly when the employee is dealing with customers. At least a peer's feedback will provide a different perspective.

Subordinate feedback can be extremely useful to supervisors and managers when addressing customer service goals. Most often the front-line employees who have direct contact with customers can offer valid and helpful feedback on group, team, or individual performance. For example, at AT&T Bell Laboratories Administrative Systems, the management team performs an annual assessment of the business head's effectiveness (called "upward feedback") which is discussed by the team and used by the business head to improve his efforts to provide high-quality customer service (Bailey et al., 1993).

The Environmental Protection Agency's Region 9 in San Francisco also developed an upward evaluation questionnaire that was first used in 1986 to open communications between employees and supervisors, to promote performance improvement in supervisors, and to empower employees by showing them that their opinions mattered. The results of the evaluation are used for feedback and developmental purposes only.

Obtaining Customer Feedback.

Soliciting customer feedback on agency performance can be done through the use of customer surveys, customer visits, a complaint system, customer focus groups, a survey of front-line employees, and other measurement mechanisms mentioned in the section of this paper on measurement. For gathering customer feedback at the individual level, however, several factors need to be taken into consideration.

First, as mentioned above, is the work a type that is appropriate for gathering customer feedback or does the nature of the work tend to produce low performance ratings from customers, no matter how the employee performed? If the work does not lend itself to direct customer feedback for individuals, indirect feedback measured at the group or agency level might be best.

Second, do customers know how individuals perform, or are they only aware of their satisfaction with the final product or service? If they have no knowledge of individual performance, they should not be used as sources of feedback on individuals but could be used for product or service satisfaction information.

Third, are customers internal or external? Many employees do not have direct contact with external customers (outside the agency). It is often easier and more appropriate to solicit feedback from internal customers, especially for administrative support positions such as personnel management specialists, office automation clerks, or budget analysts. Also, asking external customers to rate employees may make customers feel uncomfortable.

Example of an Organization's Use of Internal Customer Feedback.

Berlex Laboratories, a U.S. subsidiary of the German corporation Schering AG, had to reorganize due to a merger. Berlex conducted a study to see how they could improve internal work processes. This included interviewing internal customers. For example, questions asked about their Finance Office included, "How satisfied are you with the products and services you receive?" and "How important are those products and services to the effectiveness of your operation and to your ability to serve external customers?" Asking their internal customers these types of questions gave a signal to the whole organization that improving performance is important and that the company wanted to support its employees in providing high-quality customer service to internal as well as external customers. Internal customers gave suggestions that improved the internal operations of the organization. They also identified emerging needs that hadn't been considered (Azzolini and Shillaber, 1993).

Component ④: Recognition and Rewards

Recognizing and rewarding desired levels of customer service is a fourth component of a customer-focused performance management program. Performance management should provide built-in incentives that will promote high-quality customer service. Gainsharing, small group incentives, or goalsharing are a few examples of incentive programs that can incorporate customer service into the payout formula. Other incentives could be additional training, higher employee involvement in decisions on how the work gets done, or other things that employees value. Rewarding and recognizing outstanding customer service shows employees that the agency cares about customer service and promotes goal accomplishment.

When strategic plans are established to implement customer service standards at an organizational level, agencies would be wise to address reward and recognition programs for teams and individuals as part of that plan to support and promote the goals they are establishing. For example, as part of its strategic plans, the Health Care Financing Administration (HCFA) has established an entire incentive awards program designed to encourage employees to achieve their customer service goals.

Monetary Incentives.

When goal setting and monetary incentives are combined, the increase in performance is dramatic. Locke and Latham (1984) found a potential median increase in performance of more than 40 percent. Money supports performance improvement through goal setting by these mechanisms:

* Money can increase goal acceptance or goal commitment,

* Money can induce people to set goals, and

* A monetary incentive can lead to the setting of higher goals than would be set in the absence of a monetary incentive.

An example of an agency using monetary incentives to promote its custer service goals comes from the Tennessee Valley Authority (TVA). TVA has established an incentive program called Success Sharing. Payment of a Success Sharing award depends on whether the Agency meets its goals, which are set in three key performance areas: financial, employee worklife, and customer service. The three goals set for customer service are:

1. Achieve plant availability of at least 182 billion kilowatts per hour.

2. Achieve transmission reliability of 9.5 minutes or less of power loss per customer per month.

3. Enhance services to customers through a 5 percent reduction of administrative costs. (TVA believes that meeting this goal will help it enhance service to the Valley communities.)

TVA has established these measures as key quality indicators of customer service. The Agency must meet its financial and employee worklife goals and at least two of the three customer service goals before any awards are given. The award pool for 1993 was equal to 7.5 percent of the difference between fiscal year 1993 actual adjusted operating income and Success Sharing's financial baseline of $412 million. The pool was shared among the total number of eligible employees.

Another example of customer service incentives comes from the U.S. Marine Corps Exchange, a series of nonappropriated fund retail operations established to serve Marines and their families stationed all over the world. The Exchange has an award called the Cashier of the Quarter. During a ceremony for all employees, a $50 award is given to the cashier who has demonstrated the most outstanding customer service during the period, as determined by management using customer input. Although the amount of the gift is not large, the recognition from management and the standing ovation given by peers has made the award popular with employees. It has also put an emphasis on high-quality customer service and gives employees performance models to emulate.

Nonmonetary Recognition.

Nonmonetary recognition of employee and team achievements of customer service goals often can be more valued by employees and be more significant at improving performance than monetary awards. For example, at IBM Corporation, goal attainment is followed by immediate rewards, some monetary, some nonmonetary. Employees state that the most cherished reward is not money, however, but having one's name on the bulletin board with a notation saying "100 percent," or having a party thrown on one's behalf, or receiving a flow of congratulatory notes from superiors (Locke and Latham, 1984).

The Naval Aviation Supply Office in Philadelphia has a nonmonetary award that specifically supports customer service performance. The award is called the semi-annual Group/Team Recognition for Satisfying Internal Customers/Suppliers. It recognizes a group's special efforts in satisfying internal customers. In a recent survey, 79 percent of employees approved of this award and recommended that this form of recognition continue.

Connections Across Components

Performance management maximizes its effectiveness when the four component processes of goal setting, measurement, feedback, and recognition and reward are linked together. Throughout this paper some of these connections have been noted and bear repeating here.

Goal Setting and Measurement. To determine whether a goal has been achieved, a measurement system must be in place. If you can't quantify or verify performance in reaching the goal, there will be no way to assess levels of performance or specify where improvement is needed. Only by measuring customer service will an agency know if it is meeting its customer service standards. Only by measuring individual and team performance will managers and team members know where improvement is needed.

Goal Setting and Feedback. Feedback is most effective when it addresses performance related to goal achievement efforts. When goal setting takes place as a result of feedback on performance, employee performance improves significantly. Feedback that is vague, or that occurs either after goal achievement or after failure to reach the goal will be too late to improve performance.

Goal Setting and Rewards. Establishing incentive programs can encourage individuals and groups to set higher goals than otherwise would have been set. Incentives also increase goal acceptance by employees.

Measurement and Feedback. Establishing a measurement system without sharing that information with the employees who

could use the data to improve performance is a waste of time and energy. Effective feedback should contain information from a good measurement system. The easiest way to keep feedback specific is to use information from the measurement system.

Measurement and Rewards. In order for incentive plans to succeed, they must be based on a credible and accepted performance measurement system. And one of the most effective ways to stimulate interest in the customer service measures is to link them to rewards.

Feedback and Rewards. Feedback on goal attainment from peers and management is often a form of recognition in itself. And likewise, receiving formal recognition is a powerful form of feedback.

Improving Customer Service.

The process links mentioned here are only examples of how the processes work together to improve customer service. Connellan and Zemke (1993) perhaps best summarize the results of linking these four components in the following statement:

"...*if you set both a standard and a goal; if you involve individuals or teams in setting their targets; if you empower individuals and teams to make decisions on their own; if you combine goal setting with measurements of customer satisfaction tracked back to both individuals and teams; if you add positive coaching; if you celebrate progress; and if you use regular positive reinforcement for the right set of behaviors, then goal setting is a powerful, positive tool for sustaining Knock Your Socks Off Service.*"

Summary and Observations

Improving customer service is not only a requirement for Federal agencies, it is a necessity in these days of budget cuts and decreasing public satisfaction with Federal services. Private industry has centered its efforts on customer satisfaction as a survival technique in the world market. The Malcolm Baldrige Award was established to recognize American companies that were doing an exceptional job providing quality services and products to their customers. One of its core values is customer-driven quality, stating that the goals of companies should be customer satisfaction, customer satisfaction relative to competitors, and customer retention, among other things. In fact, 30 percent of the award is weighted on customer satisfaction alone.

With the increased emphasis on customer satisfaction, Federal agencies need tools to help them achieve their customer service goals. The performance management program an agency establishes can be an important tool for aligning and setting customer service goals and standards, for establishing measurement and feedback processes, and for recognizing and rewarding high-quality customer service. As one manager observed: "People perform best when they know what is expected of them. Add authority to clearly stated management expectations with consistent measurement and follow up, and you can get the results you are looking for." (Lindo, 1993.)

Finally, agencies simply will not reach the President's goal of best-in-business customer service unless they take action by setting organizational and individual customer service standards and goals. "Reacting quickly to customers' problems might be considered good customer service, but continued fire-fighting rarely leads to customer satisfaction. An entire company [or agency] must be dedicated to the goal of providing proactive customer service." (Skrabec, 1993).

Appendix 1

THE WHITE HOUSE

EXECUTIVE ORDER NO. 12862
SETTING CUSTOMER SERVICE STANDARDS

Putting people first means ensuring that the Federal Government provides the highest quality service possible to the American people. Public officials must embark upon a revolution within the Federal Government to change the way it does business. This will require continual reform of the executive branch's management practices and operations to provide service to the public that matches or exceeds the best service available in the private sector.

NOW, THEREFORE, to establish and implement customer service standards to guide the operations of the executive branch, and by the authority vested in me as President by the Constitution and the laws of the United States, it is hereby ordered:

Section 1. Customer Service Standards. In order to carry out the principles of the National Performance Review, the Federal Government must be customer-driven. The standard of quality for services provided to the public shall be: Customer service equal to the best in business. For the purposes of this order, "customer" shall mean an individual or entity who is directly served by a department or agency. "Best in business" shall mean the highest quality of service delivered to customers by private organizations providing a comparable or analogous service.

All executive departments and agencies (hereinafter referred to collectively as "agency" or "agencies") that provide significant services directly to the public shall provide those services in a manner that seeks to meet the customer service standard established herein and shall take the following actions:

(a) identify the customers who are, or should be, served by the agency;

(b) survey customers to determine the kind and quality of services they want and their level of satisfaction with existing services;

(c) post service standards and measure results against them;

(d) benchmark customer service performance against the best in business;

(e) survey front-line employees on barriers to, and ideas for, matching the best in business;

(f) provide customers with choices in both the sources of service and the means of delivery;

(g) make information, services, and complaint systems easily accessible; and

(h) provide means to address customer complaints.

Sec. 2. Report on Customer Service Surveys. By March 8, 1994, each agency subject to this order shall report on its customer surveys to the President. As information about customer satisfaction becomes available, each agency shall use that information in judging the performance of agency management and in making resource allocations.

Sec. 3. Customer Service Plans. By September 8, 1994, each agency subject to this order shall publish a customer service plan that can be readily understood by its customers. The plan shall include customer service standards and describe future plans for customer surveys. It also shall identify the private and public sector standards that the agency used to benchmark its performance against the best in business. In connection with the plan, each agency is encouraged to provide training resources for programs needed by employees who directly serve customers and by managers making use of customer survey information to promote the principles and objectives contained herein.

Sec. 4. Independent Agencies. Independent agencies are requested to adhere to this order.

Sec. 5. Judicial Review. This order is for the internal management of the executive branch and does not create any right or benefit, substantive or procedural, enforceable by a party against the United States, its agencies or instrumentalities, its officers or employees, or any other person.

WILLIAM J. CLINTON

THE WHITE HOUSE,

September 11, 1993

Appendix 2

**The White House
Washington**

March 22, 1995

MEMORANDUM FOR HEADS OF EXECUTIVE DEPARTMENTS AND
AGENCIES

SUBJECT: **Improving Customer Service**

In the first phase of this Administration's reinventing government initiative, I
established the principle that government must be customer-driven. Executive
Order No. 12862, "Setting Customer Service Standards," called for a revolution within the Federal Government to change the way it does business. The
initial agency responses to that order, including the service standards published
in September 1994, have begun the process of establishing a more customer-
focused government. For the first time, the Federal Government's customers
have been told what they have a right to expect when they ask for service.

In the second phase of reinventing government ("Phase II"), this effort should
be continued and integrated with other restructuring activities. The first
question agency restructuring teams should ask is whether a program or
function is critical to the agency's missions based on "customer" input. To
carry out this Phase II effort and assure that government puts the customer
first, I am now directing the additional steps set forth in this memorandum.

   <u>Actions.</u> The agencies covered by Executive Order No. 12862 are directed
as follows:

   1. In order to continue customer service reform, agencies shall treat the
requirements of Executive Order No. 12862 as continuing requirements. The
actions the order prescribes, such as surveying customers, surveying employees,
and bench marking, shall be continuing agency activities. The purpose of
these actions will remain as indicated in Executive Order No. 12862   the
establishment and implementation of customer service standards to guide the
operations of the executive branch.

2. Agencies shall, by September 1, 1995, complete the publication of customer service standards, in a form readily available to customers, for all operations that deliver significant services directly to the public. This shall include services that are delivered in partnership with State and local governments, services delivered by small agencies and regulatory agencies, and customer services of enforcement agencies.

3. Agencies shall, on an ongoing basis, measure results achieved against the customer service standards and report those results to customers at least annually. Reports should be in terms readily understood by individual customers. Public reports shall be made beginning no later than September 15, 1995. Measurement systems should include objective measures wherever possible, but should also include customer satisfaction as a measure. Customer views should be obtained to determine whether standards have been set on what matters most to the customer. Agencies should publish replacement standards if needed to reflect these views.

4. Development and tracking of customer service measures, standards, and performance should be integrated with other performance initiatives, including Phase II restructuring. Customer service standards also should be related to legislative activities, including strategic planning and performance measurement under the Government Performance and Results Act of 1993, reporting on financial and program performance under the Chief Financial Officers Act of 1990, and the Government Management and Reform Act of 1994. Operating plans, regulations and guidelines, training programs, and personnel classification and evaluation systems should be aligned with a customer focus.

5. Agencies shall continue to survey employees on ideas to improve customer service, take action to motivate and recognize employees for meeting or exceeding customer service standards, and for promoting customer service. Without satisfied employees, we cannot have satisfied customers.

6. Agencies should initiate and support actions that cut across agency lines to serve shared customer groups. Agencies should take steps to develop cross-agency, one-stop service to customer groups, so their customers do not needlessly go from one agency to another. Where possible, these steps should take advantage of new information technology tools to achieve results.

The standard of quality we seek from these actions and the Executive order is customer service for the American people that is equal to the best in business.

Independent Agencies. Independent agencies are requested to adhere to this directive.

Judicial Review. This directive is for the internal management of the executive branch and does not create any right or benefit, substantive or procedural, enforceable by a party against the United States, its agencies or instrumentalities, its officers or employees, or any other person.

WILLIAM J. CLINTON

Major Contributor
to This Report

Karen Lebing
Personnel Management Specialist
U.S. Office of Personnel Management
Office of Employee Relations and Workforce Performance
Performance Management and Incentive Awards Division

Bibliography

Azzolini, Mary and James Schillaber, "Internal Service Quality: Winning From the Inside Out," *Quality Progress*, November 1993, pages 75-78.

Bailey, Marvin, Gary Bragar, April Cormaci, Colleen Murray, and Cal Paranteau, "Recipes for Disaster," *Quality Progress*, January 1993, pages 55-58.

Carson, Paula Phillips and Kerry Carson, "Managing Creativity Enhancement Through Goal-Setting and Feedback," *Journal of Creative Behavior*, January-March 1993, pages 36-45.

Connellan, Thomas K. and Ron Zemke, *Sustaining Knock Your Socks Off Service*, New York, NY: American Management Association, 1993.

Easton, George S., "The 1993 State of U.S. Total Quality Management: A Baldrige Examiner's Perspective," *California Management Review*, Spring 1993, pages 32-54.

Flanagan, Theresa A. and Joan O. Fredericks, "Improving Company Performance through Customer-Satisfaction Measurement and Management," *National Productivity Review*, Spring 1993, pages 239-258.

Goodman, John A., "Preventing TQM Problems: Measured Steps Toward Customer-Driven Quality Improvement," *National Productivity Review*, Autumn 1993, pages 555-571.

Graessel, Bob and Pete Zeidler, "Using Quality Function Deployment to Improve Customer Service," *Quality Progress*, November 1993, pages 59-63.

Lindo, David K., "How Much Rope Do You Need?," *Supervision*, October 1993, pages 3-4.

Locke, E.A. & G.P. Latham, *Goal Setting: A Motivational Technique That Works*, Englewood Cliffs, NJ: Prentice Hall, 1984.

Meyer, Christopher, "How the Right Measures Help Teams Excel," *Harvard Business Review*, May-June 1994, pages 95-103.

Skrabeck, Jr., Quentin R., "Get All Employees Involved in Satisfying Customers," *Quality Progress*, November 1993, pages 87-89.

Wilson, Liz, "The Quality Measure is Customer Opinion," *Journal for Quality & Participation*, October/November 1993, pages 12-14.

Zigon, Jack, "Making Performance Appraisal Work For Teams," *Training*, June 1994, pages 5863.

www.ingramcontent.com/pod-product-compliance
Lightning Source LLC
Chambersburg PA
CBHW081417170526

45166CB00010B/3384